BART SIMPSON

CLASS CLOWN

HARPER

NEW YORK • LONDON • TORONTO • SYDNEY

BART SIMPSON: CLASS CLOWN

Collects Bart Simpson Comics 33, 34, 35, 36, 37

FIRST EDITION

ISBN 978-0-06-197629-2

10 11 12 13 14 WCP 10 9 8 7 6 5 4 3 2 1

Publisher: Matt Groening
Creative Director: Bill Morrison
Managing Editor: Terry Delegeane
Director of Operations: Robert Zaugh
Art Director: Nathan Kane
Art Director Special Projects: Serban Cristescu
Production Manager: Christopher Ungar
Assistant Art Director: Chia-Hsien Jason Ho
Production/Design: Karen Bates, Nathan Hamill, Art Villanueva
Staff Artist: Mike Rote
Administration: Ruth Waytz, Pete Benson
Legal Guardian: Susan A. Grode

Trade Paperback Concepts and Design: Serban Cristescu

Cover: Kevin Newman and Serban Cristescu

HarperCollins Editors: Hope Innelli, Jeremy Cesarec

Contributing Artists:
Marcos Asprec, Karen Bates, John Costanza, Serban Cristescu, Mike DeCarlo,
Frances Dinglasan, Nathan Hamill , Jason Ho, Nathan Kane, Earl Kress, James Lloyd, Bill Morrison,
Kevin Newman, Joey Nilges, Phyllis Novin, Phil Ortiz, Andrew Pepoy, Mike Rote, Howard Shum,
Steve Steere Jr., Chris Ungar, Carlos Valenti, Art Villanueva

Contributing Writers:
James W. Bates, Tony DiGerolamo, Chuck Dixon, Clay & Susan Griffith,
Tom Peyer, Ty Templeton, Mary Trainor

Printed by World Color Press, Inc, Montreal, QC, Canada. 04/06/2010

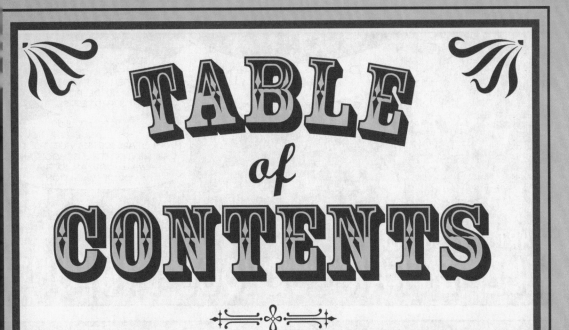

TABLE of CONTENTS

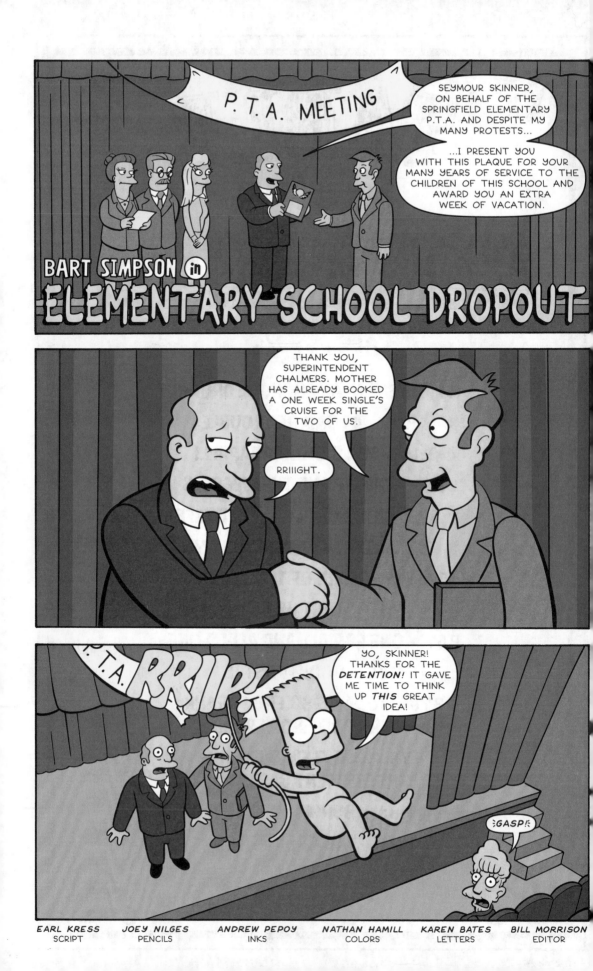

P.T.A. MEETING

SEYMOUR SKINNER, ON BEHALF OF THE SPRINGFIELD ELEMENTARY P.T.A. AND DESPITE MY MANY PROTESTS...

...I PRESENT YOU WITH THIS PLAQUE FOR YOUR MANY YEARS OF SERVICE TO THE CHILDREN OF THIS SCHOOL AND AWARD YOU AN EXTRA WEEK OF VACATION.

BART SIMPSON in ELEMENTARY SCHOOL DROPOUT

THANK YOU, SUPERINTENDENT CHALMERS. MOTHER HAS ALREADY BOOKED A ONE WEEK SINGLE'S CRUISE FOR THE TWO OF US.

RRIIIGHT.

P.T.A. RRIIP!

YO, SKINNER! THANKS FOR THE *DETENTION!* IT GAVE ME TIME TO THINK UP *THIS* GREAT IDEA!

¡GASP!

EARL KRESS SCRIPT *JOEY NILGES* PENCILS *ANDREW PEPOY* INKS *NATHAN HAMILL* COLORS *KAREN BATES* LETTERS *BILL MORRISON* EDITOR

7

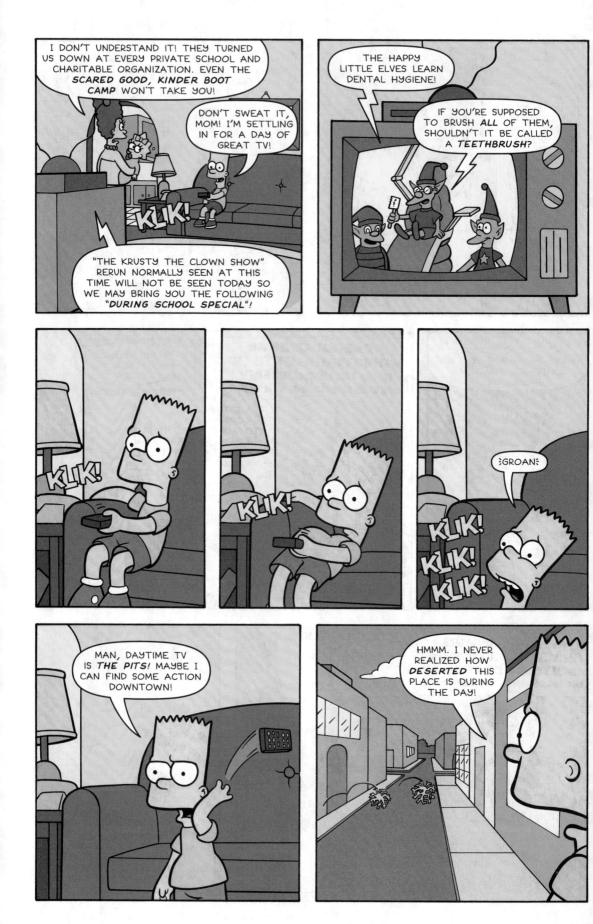

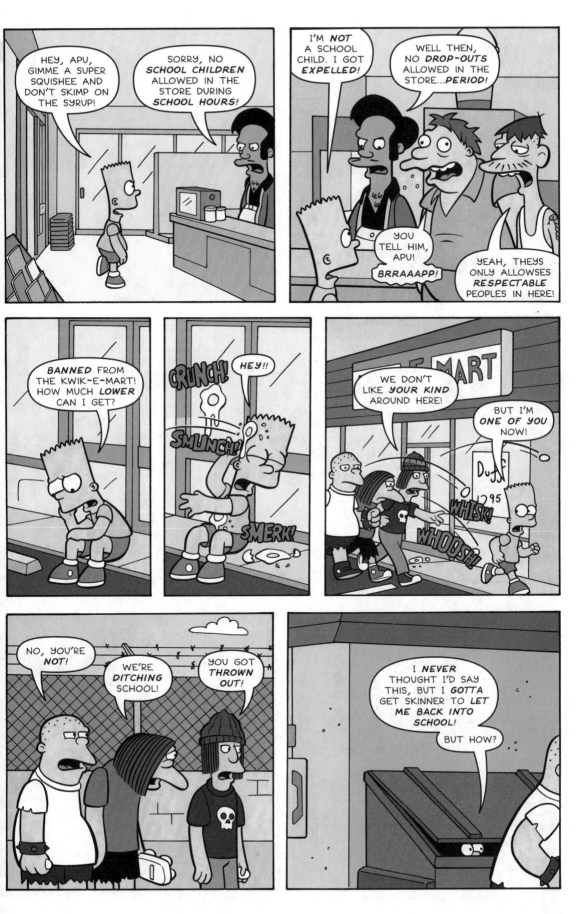

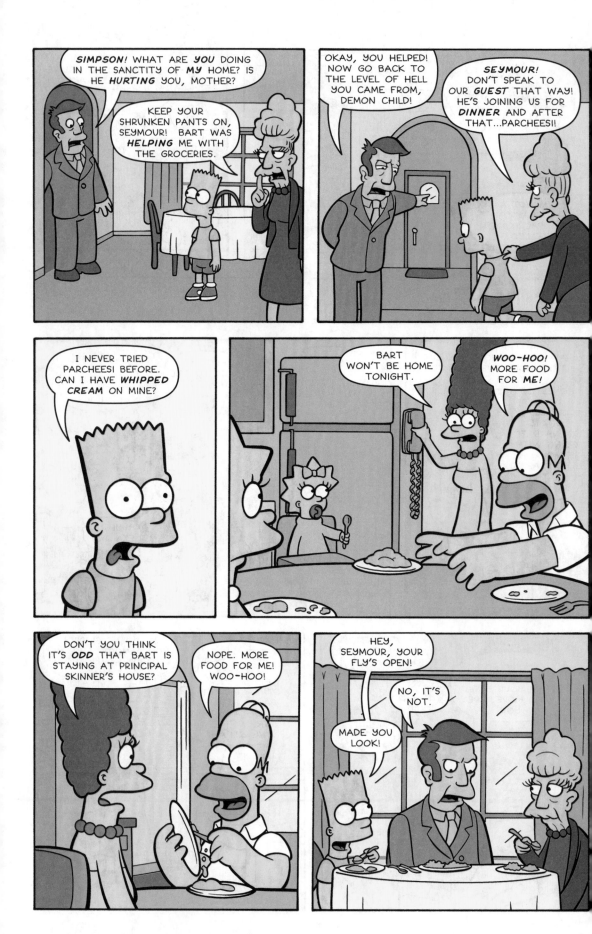

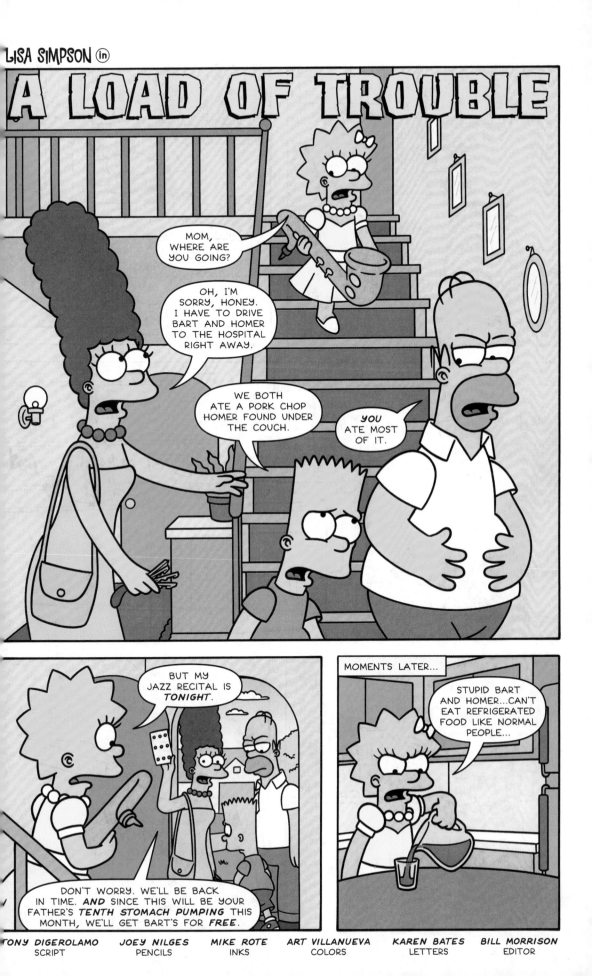

LISA SIMPSON in

A LOAD OF TROUBLE

MOM, WHERE ARE YOU GOING?

OH, I'M SORRY, HONEY. I HAVE TO DRIVE BART AND HOMER TO THE HOSPITAL RIGHT AWAY.

WE BOTH ATE A PORK CHOP HOMER FOUND UNDER THE COUCH.

YOU ATE MOST OF IT.

BUT MY JAZZ RECITAL IS *TONIGHT*.

DON'T WORRY. WE'LL BE BACK IN TIME. *AND* SINCE THIS WILL BE YOUR FATHER'S *TENTH STOMACH PUMPING* THIS MONTH, WE'LL GET BART'S FOR *FREE*.

MOMENTS LATER...

STUPID BART AND HOMER...CAN'T EAT REFRIGERATED FOOD LIKE NORMAL PEOPLE...

TONY DIGEROLAMO
SCRIPT

JOEY NILGES
PENCILS

MIKE ROTE
INKS

ART VILLANUEVA
COLORS

KAREN BATES
LETTERS

BILL MORRISON
EDITOR

25

"IT WAS THE HEY DAY OF WEASELMANIA!"

"WE HAD DUNCAN MCGREGOR ON THE BASS GUITAR..."

I'M THE WILY, WHEEDLING WEASEL!

"ANGUS MCDUFF ON LEAD GUITAR..."

I'M THE WEAK, WIMPY WEASEL!

"GEORDIE MCINTYRE ON THE BAGPIPES..."

I'M THE WEIRD, WHEEZY WEASEL!

"AND ME, WEE WILLIE, ON THE DRUMS."

I'M THE WISE, WITTY WEASEL!

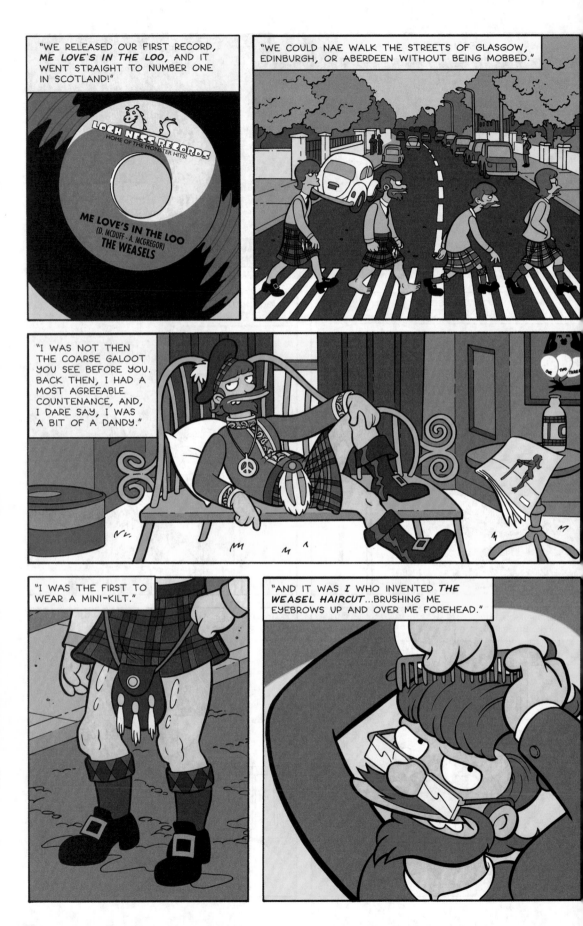

"WE RELEASED OUR FIRST RECORD, *ME LOVE'S IN THE LOO*, AND IT WENT STRAIGHT TO NUMBER ONE IN SCOTLAND!"

LOCH NESS RECORDS
HOME OF THE MONSTER HITS!

ME LOVE'S IN THE LOO
(D. MCDUFF - A. MCGREGOR)
THE WEASELS

"WE COULD NAE WALK THE STREETS OF GLASGOW, EDINBURGH, OR ABERDEEN WITHOUT BEING MOBBED."

"I WAS NOT THEN THE COARSE GALOOT YOU SEE BEFORE YOU. BACK THEN, I HAD A MOST AGREEABLE COUNTENANCE, AND, I DARE SAY, I WAS A BIT OF A DANDY."

ONE TWO THREE

"I WAS THE FIRST TO WEAR A MINI-KILT."

"AND IT WAS *I* WHO INVENTED *THE WEASEL HAIRCUT*...BRUSHING ME EYEBROWS UP AND OVER ME FOREHEAD."

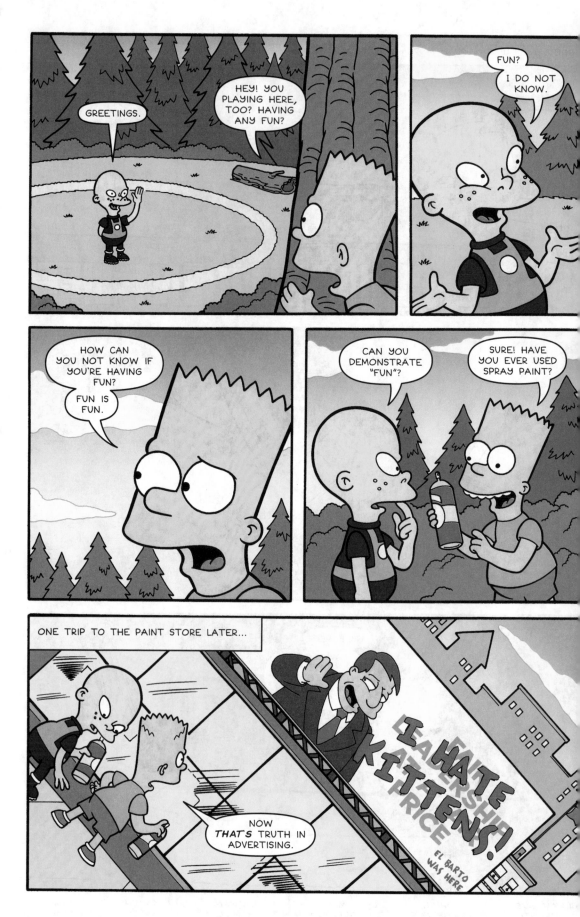

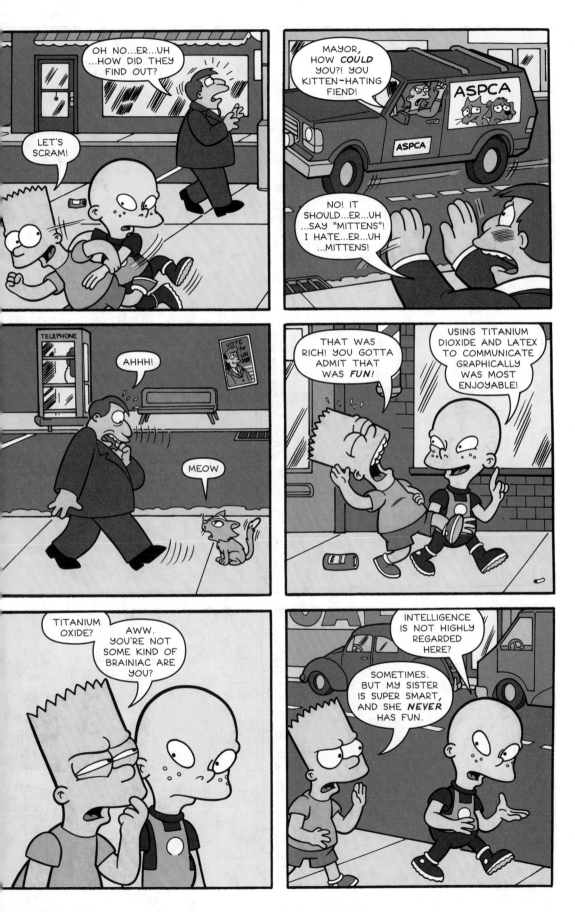

WOW!

WORST FREE COMIC BOOK DAY *EVER!*

RATS! IT'S CHIEF WIGGUM. HE COULD STOP THE FUN.

NO MORE COMICS?

NO MORE *ANYTHING!* BUT DON'T WORRY. I'VE GOT AN IDEA.

NO. NO. TURN THEM *COUNTER-CLOCKWISE.*

WAIT! ZZZZ... I'LL MARRY THAT PORK RIND!

AND THEY JUST COME OFF? AMAZING.

⁑SNORT!⁑

I DIDN'T EAT MY PORK RIND BRIDE! HONEST!

WHA--?

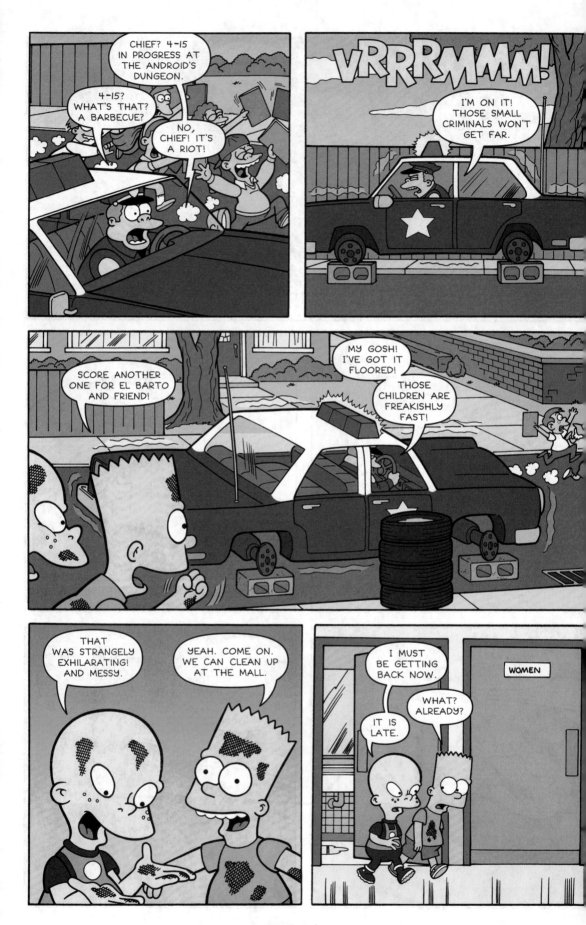

41

OM PEYER
SCRIPT

MARCOS APSREC
PENCILS

MIKE ROTE
INKS

ART VILLANUEVA
COLORS

KAREN BATES
LETTERS

BILL MORRISON
EDITOR

MATT GROENING presents

BART SIMPSON in THE RETURN OF TRUCKASAURUS

JAMES BATES
SCRIPT

CARLOS VALENTI
PENCILS

STEVE STEERE, JR.
INKS

NATHAN HAMILL
COLORS

KAREN BATES
LETTERS

BILL MORRISON
EDITOR

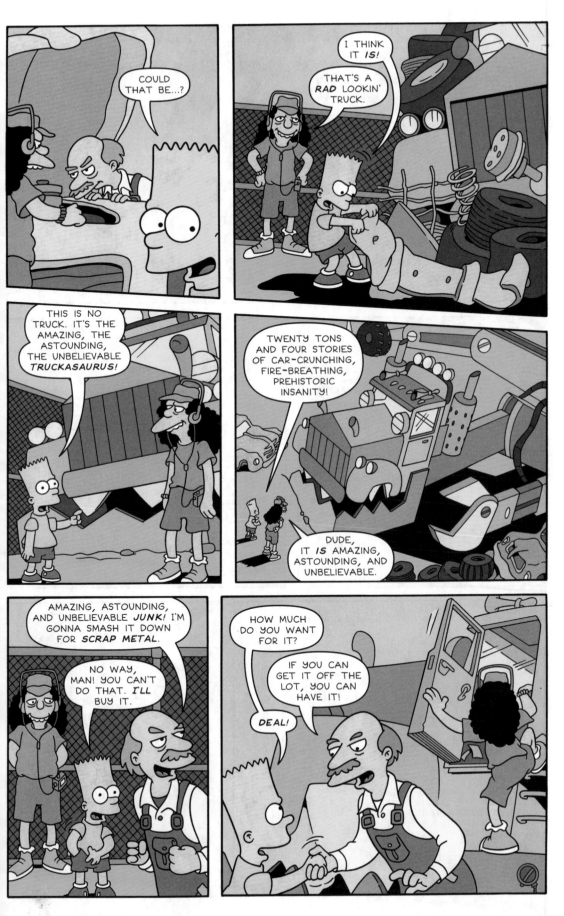

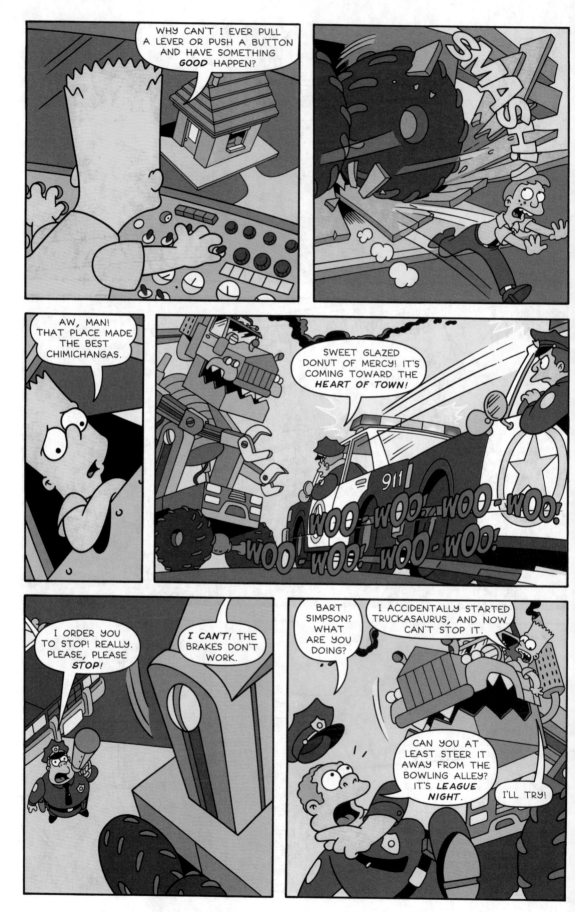

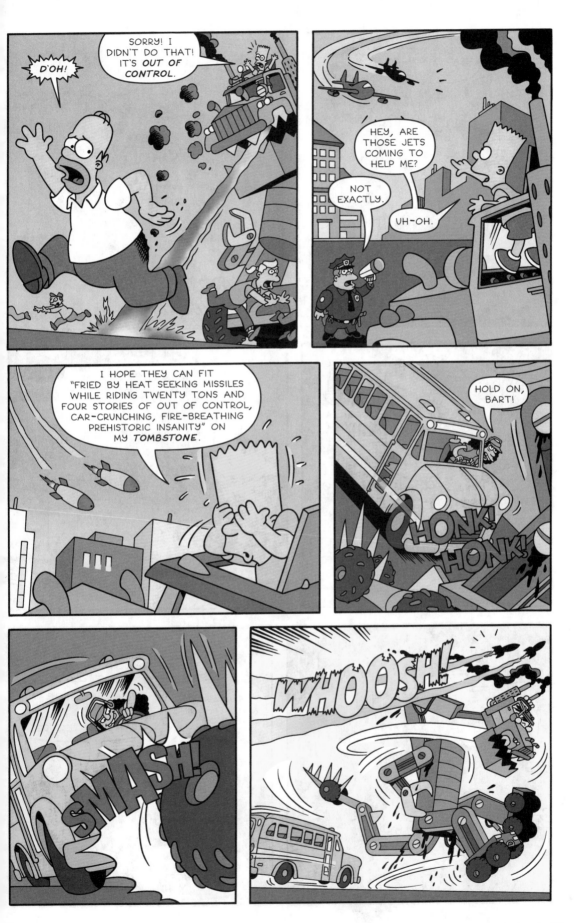

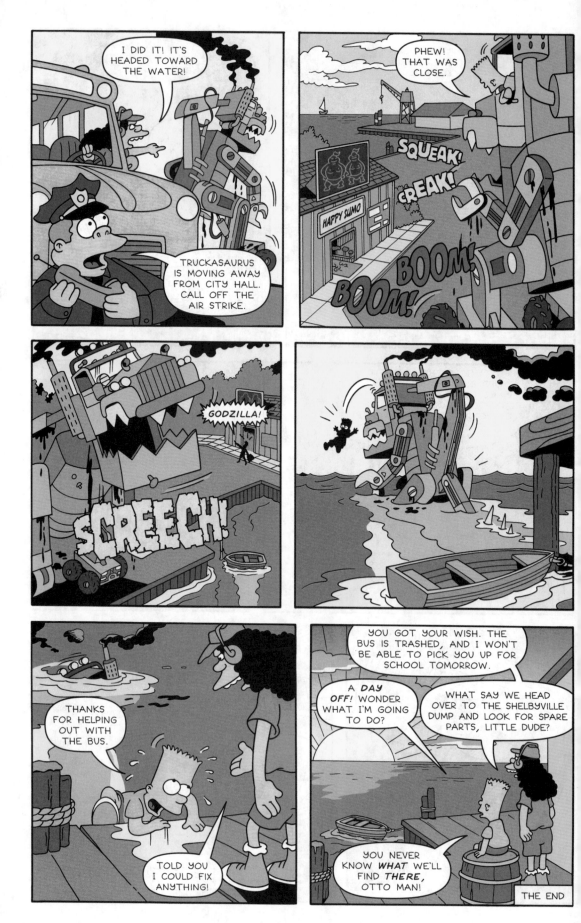

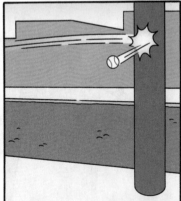

MARY TRAINOR
SCRIPT & LAYOUTS

JASON HO
PENCILS

MIKE ROTE
INKS

ART VILLANUEVA
COLORS

KAREN BATES
LETTERS

BILL MORRISON
EDITOR

THE END

MARY TRAINOR
SCRIPT

JAMES LLOYD
PENCILS

ANDREW PEPOY
INKS

NATHAN HAMILL
COLORS

KAREN BATES
LETTERS

BILL MORRISON
EDITOR

SO WHO WERE THESE GUYS AND HOW DID THEY GET LOST?

LONG, LONG AGO THERE WAS A TRIBE OF GENTLE PEOPLE LIVING PEACEFULLY IN THE FIELD OF SPRINGS...

"LEGEND HAS IT THAT THESE MEEK AND MELLOW FOLK WERE DRIVEN FROM THEIR LAND BY A FIERCE BAND OF RAPACIOUS DEVELOPERS."

"UNABLE TO QUALIFY FOR A HOME LOAN, THE TRIBE WAS FORCED TO FLEE THE FIELD OF SPRINGS."

STONEY HENGE ESTATES
-MODERN PALEOLITHIC LIVING AT ITS BEST!

"THEY DISPERSED THROUGHOUT THE LAND, HOLDING FIRM IN THE BELIEF THAT THEY WOULD RETURN SOMEDAY. IT WAS SAID THAT THE TRIBE WOULD BE LOST FOR A THOUSAND YEARS...UNTIL THEIR PROPHET RETURNED TO RETRIEVE THEIR TRIBAL BIBLE."

THIS TRIBAL BIBLE!

"...AND VERILY YOUR TRIBE SHALL REMAINETH LOST UNTIL THE CHOSEN ONE DOTH COMETH FORTH HE IS YOUR ALPHA MEN." WHOA!!! MILHOUSE AND I MUST BE THE ALPHA MEN!

POSSIBLY. BUT, THE TRIBAL BIBLE FORETELLS OF A CHOSEN ONE, NOT TWO. AMONG BABOONS, AND I USE THE TERM ADVISEDLY, THIS WOULD REFER TO THE ALPHA MALE.

59

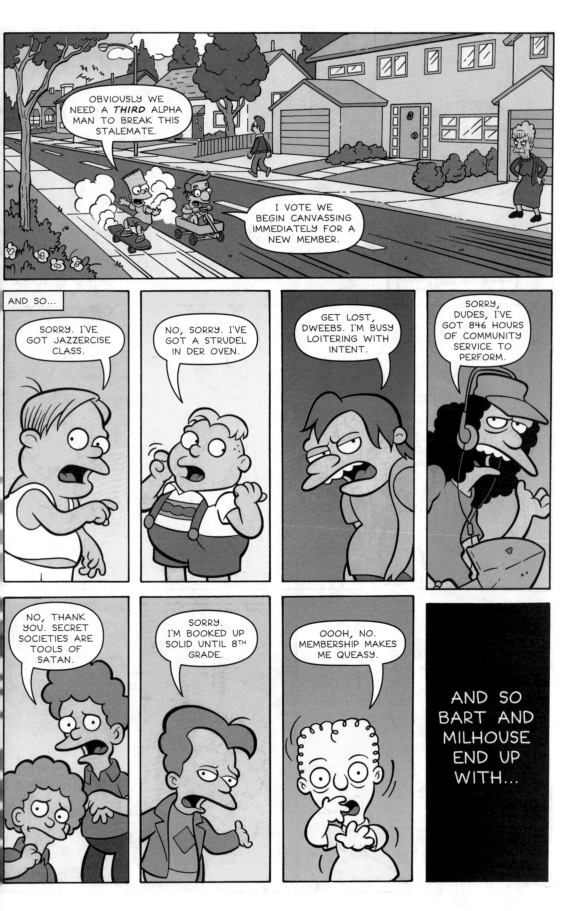

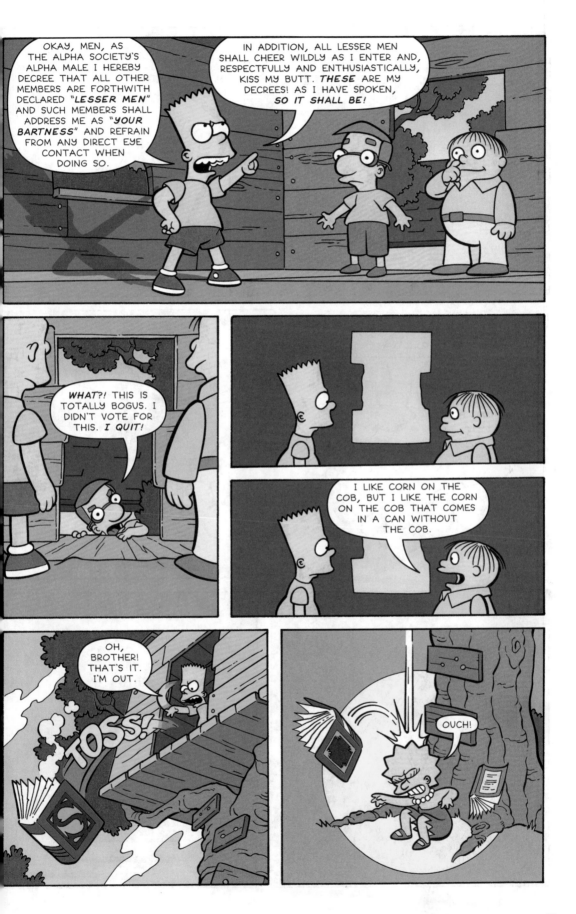

MARY TRAINOR
SCRIPT

JASON HO
PENCILS

MIKE ROTE
INKS

CHRIS UNGAR
COLORS

KAREN BATES
LETTERS

BILL MORRISON
EDITOR

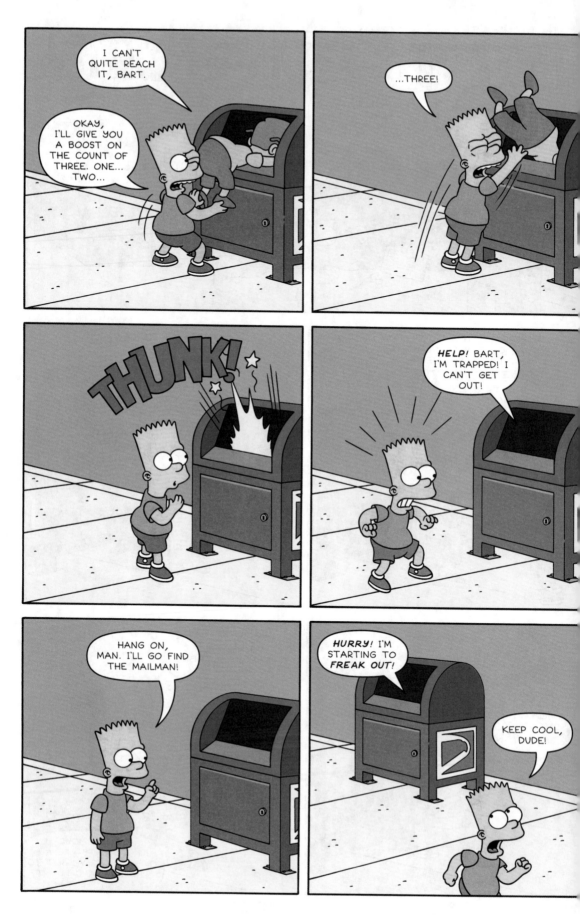

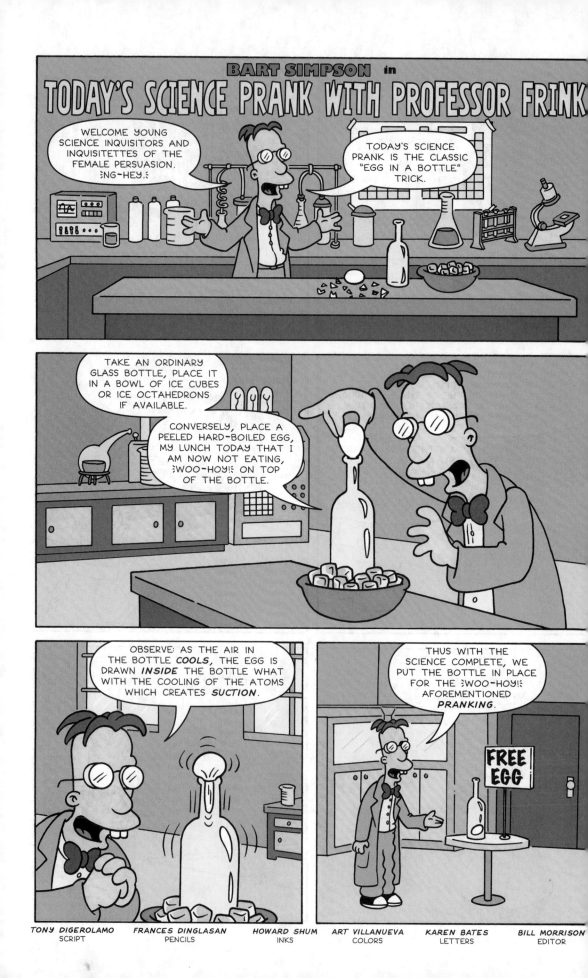

TONY DIGEROLAMO
SCRIPT

FRANCES DINGLASAN
PENCILS

HOWARD SHUM
INKS

ART VILLANUEVA
COLORS

KAREN BATES
LETTERS

BILL MORRISON
EDITOR

BART SIMPSON IN

ONE FLEW OVER THE RETIREMENT CASTLE

SPRINGFIELD RETIREMENT CASTLE

SCREEEECH!

GO ON, BOY. YOUR REPORT'S NOT GOING TO WRITE ITSELF.

CAN'T I JUST COPY STUFF OUT OF AN ENCYCLOPEDIA AND RENT A COSTUME?

IT'S NOT JUST GRAMPA. IT'S ALL THOSE OLD PEOPLE. THEY'RE DEPRESSING!

THAT'S WHY THEY'RE THE PERFECT ONES TO TALK TO ABOUT *THE GREAT DEPRESSION!*

YOU'LL BE BACK SOON, RIGHT?

SHAME ON YOU, BOY. OLD PEOPLE DESERVE YOUR RESPECT...NOW GET IN THERE SO I CAN GET AWAY BEFORE THE OLD MAN SEES ME AND I HAVE TO GO IN, TOO!

JAMES W. BATES
SCRIPT

JOEY NILGES
PENCILS

MIKE ROTE
INKS

NATHAN HAMILL
COLORS

KAREN BATES
LETTERS

BILL MORRISON
EDITOR

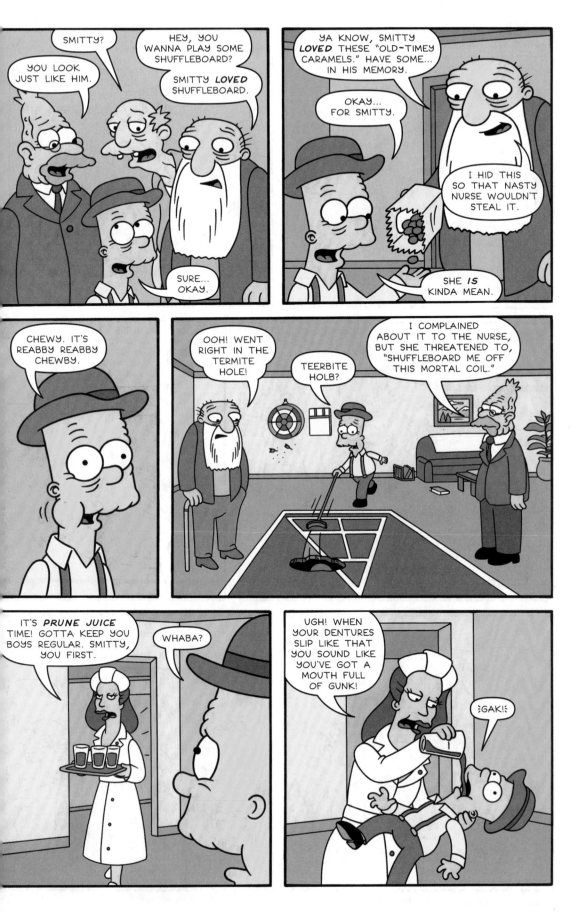

WHAT'S HAPPENED TO MY FACE? WHY DO I SMELL LIKE LINIMENT OIL?

SOMETHING WRONG, NURSE FLETCHER?

MY STOMACH!

FACE CREAM

GRR-GRR-GRR

IF YOU'RE GONNA BE SICK, YOU SHOULD PUT A HOUSE FROCK OVER YOUR PRETTY DRESS.

W-WHAT?

GRR-GRR-GRR

EAT SOME OF MY CARAMELS TO SETTLE YOUR GUTS. I KNOW YOU LIKE 'EM. YOU'VE SWIPED ENOUGH FROM ME.

;GAK!;

I'VE TURBED INTO AN OLB LABY!

YOU "TURBED" INTO A WHAT? WHEN YOUR DENTURES SLIP LIKE THAT YOU SOUND LIKE YOU'VE GOT A MOUTH FULL OF GUNK!

DING DONG!

OH NO! THAT'S MY BOYFRIEND! I CAN'T LET HIM SEE ME LIKE THIS!

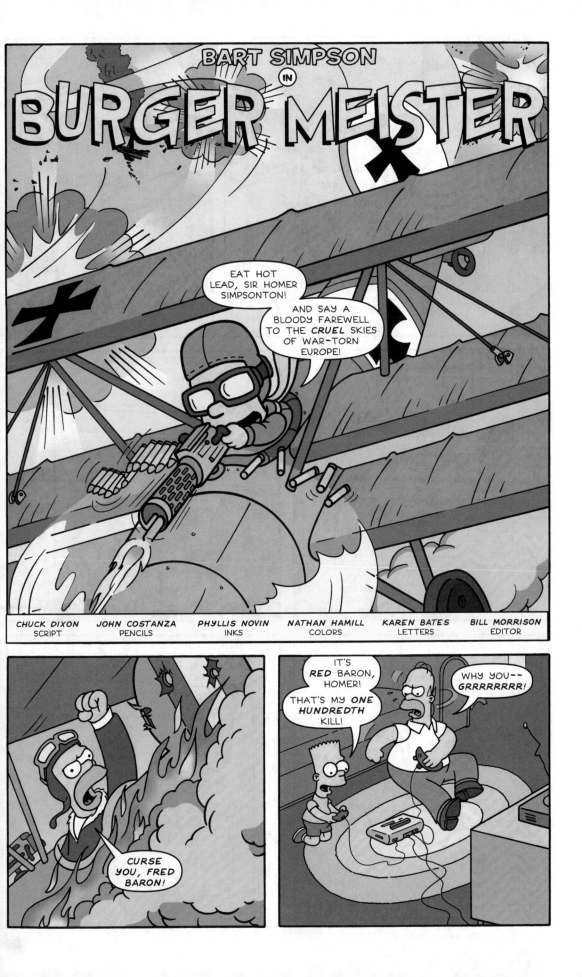

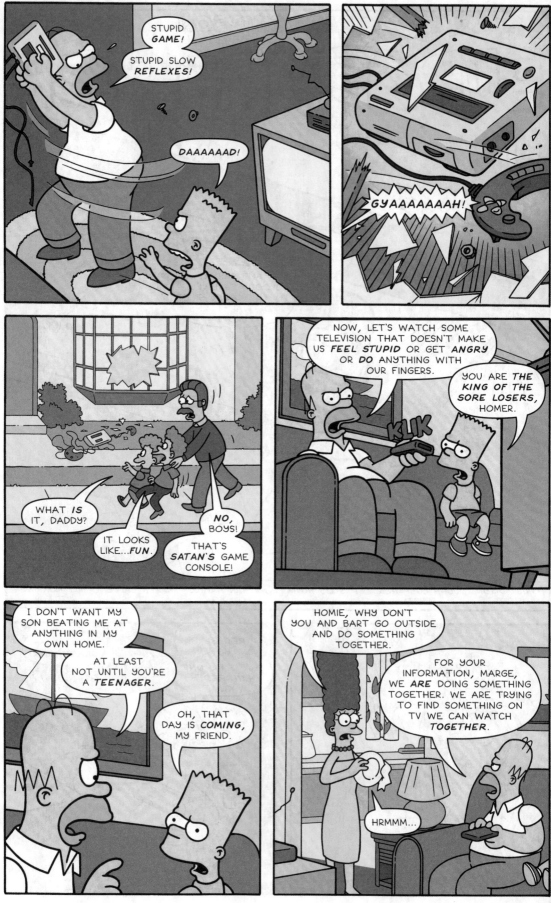

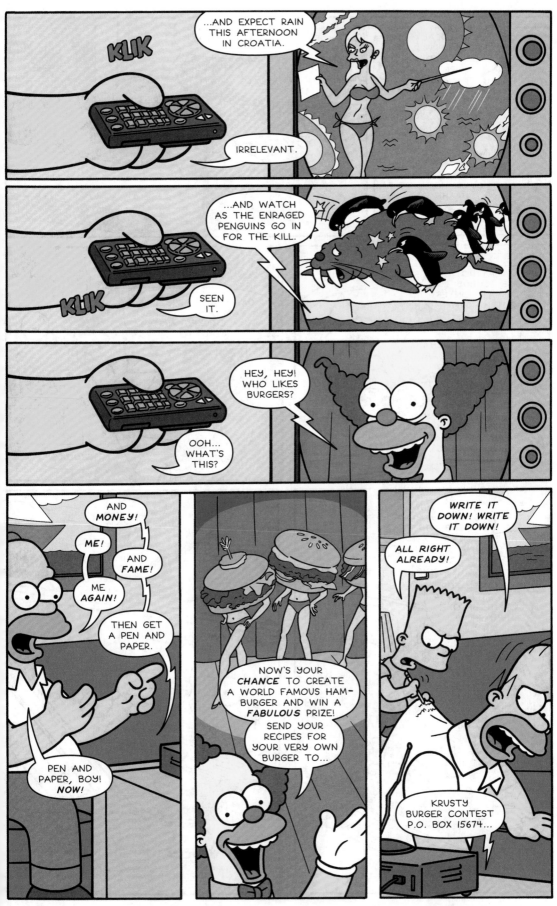

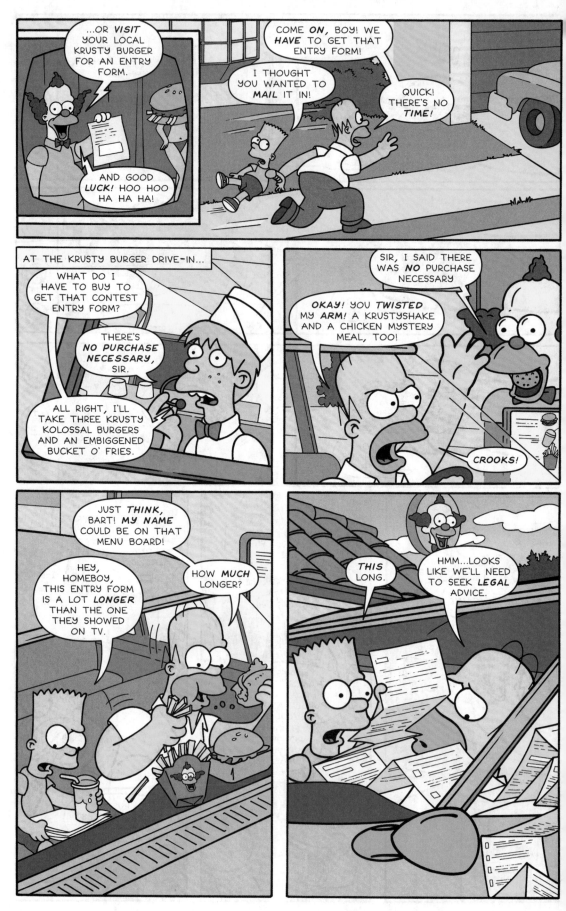

MARGE! TASTE THIS!

NOT *NOW*, HOM--

≋MMPH!≋

IS IT *GOOD*? IS IT? DO YOU *LIKE* IT? *PLEASE* LIKE IT!

≋NNMMRRMM≋

HOMER, DID YOU PUT *EGG SHELLS* IN THIS BURGER?

THEY WERE FOR *TEXTURE*! YOU WEREN'T *SUPPOSED* TO BE ABLE TO TASTE THEM!

OH, I'M A FAILURE! A FAILURE!

BAM!

BAM!

HOMIE, STOP!

YOU GET *RIGHT* BACK IN THAT KITCHEN, MISTER! I NOT GOING TO *LET* YOU GIVE UP!

AW, MARGE...

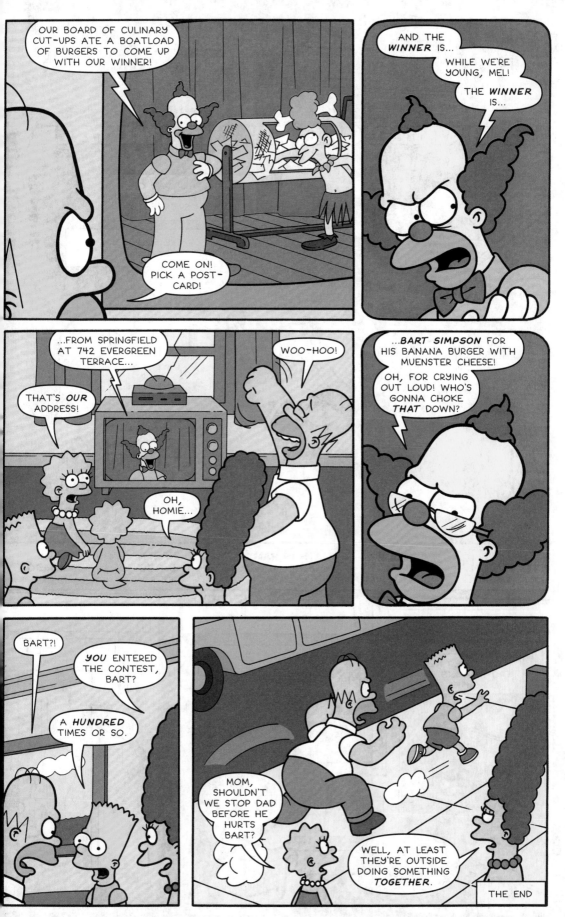

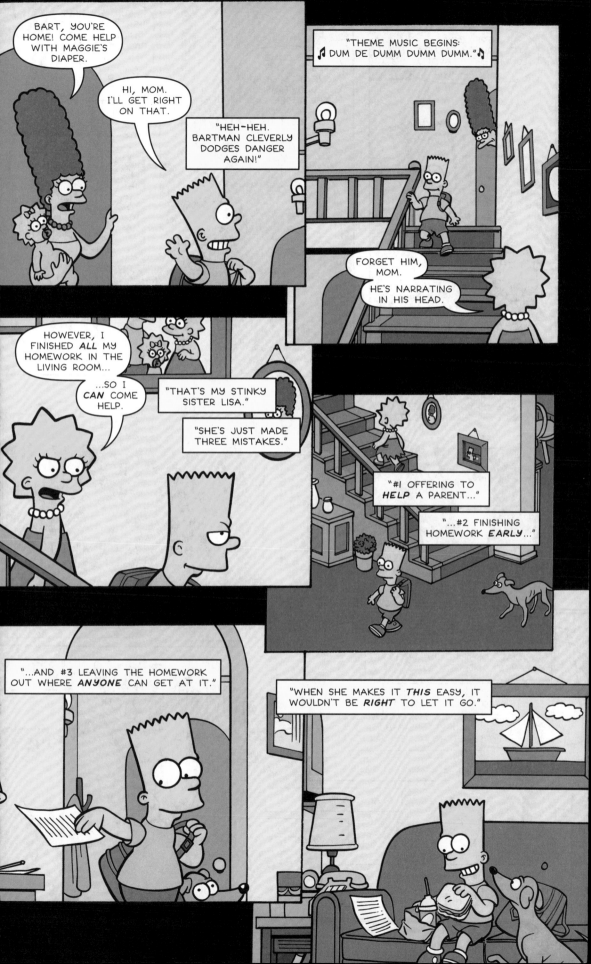

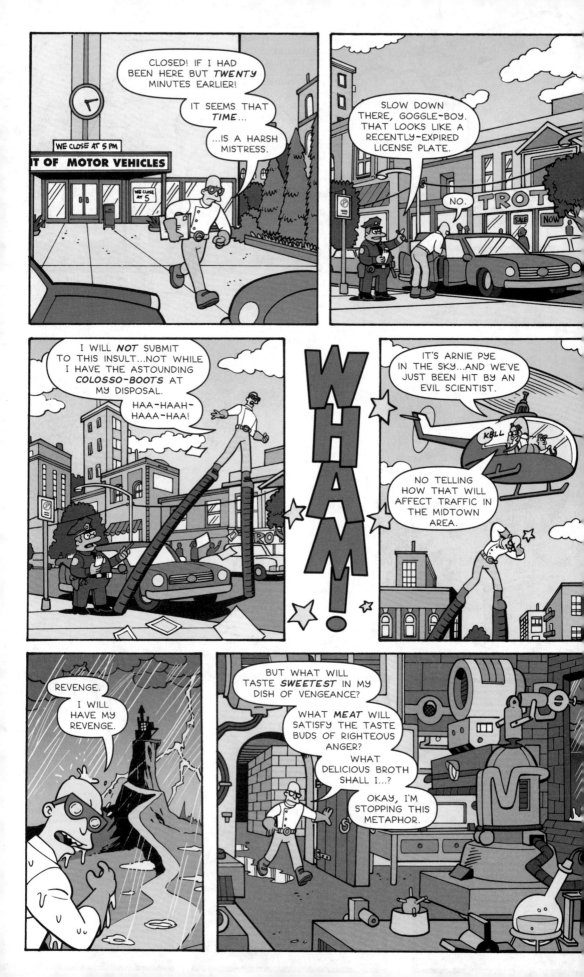

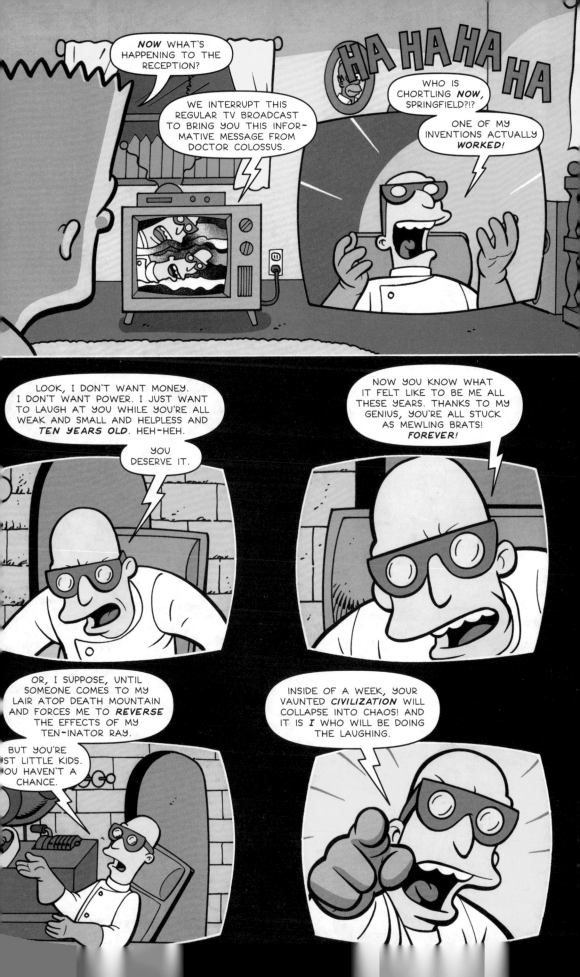

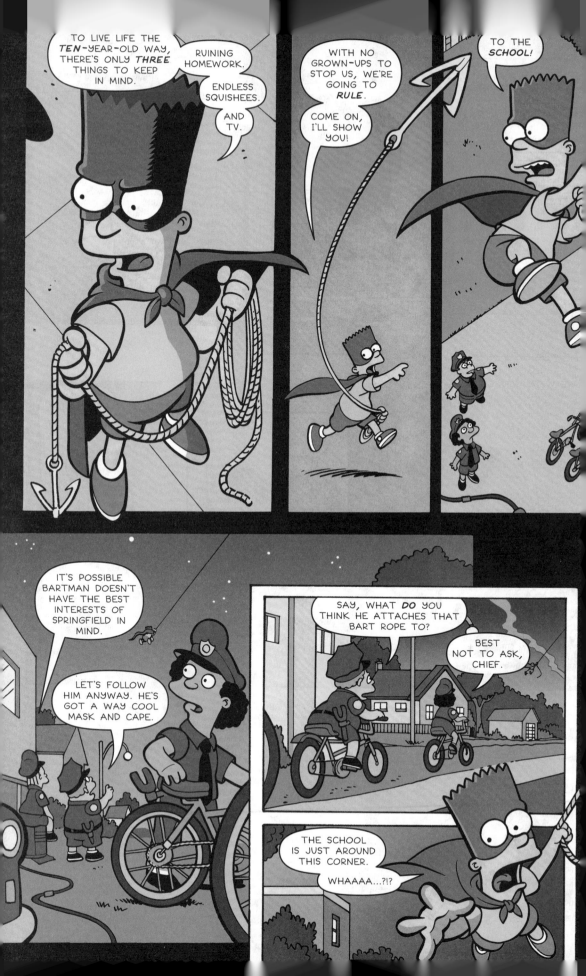

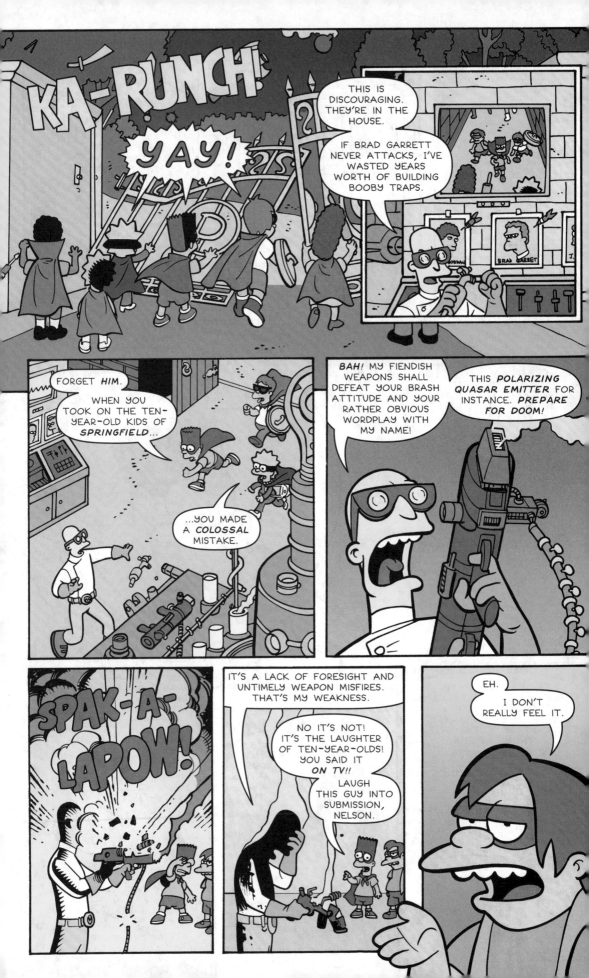